WAVING FROM SHORE

WAVING
FROM
SHORE

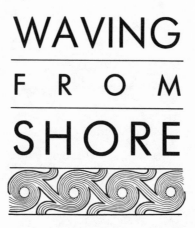

POEMS BY LISEL MUELLER

1989
LOUISIANA STATE UNIVERSITY PRESS
BATON ROUGE AND LONDON

Manufactured in the United States of America

First printing

98 97 96 95 94 93 92 91 90 89   5 4 3 2 1

Designer: Laura Roubique Gleason
Typeface: Bembo
Typesetter: G&S Typesetters, Inc.
Printer and Binder: Thomson-Shore, Inc.

Library of Congress Cataloging-in-Publication Data

Mueller, Lisel.
    Waving from shore : poems / by Lisel Mueller.
      p. cm.
    ISBN 0-8071-1575-4. — ISBN 0-8071-1576-2 (pbk.)
    I. Title.
  PS3563.U35W38 1989
  811'.54—dc20   89-12144
                                    CIP

A number of the poems published here first appeared, sometimes in slightly different form, in the following journals: *Ark River Review, The Georgia Review, New Letters, The Ohio Review, Poetry, Poetry Northwest, Quarterly West, The Southern California Anthology, The Southern Florida Poetry Review, Special Report,* and *Triquarterly.*

"Apocryphal Story" was first printed, under the title "Annals 1," in the chapbook *Life of a Queen,* published by Northeast/Juniper Books.

The paper in this book meets the guidelines for permanence and durability of the Committee on Production Guidelines for Book Longevity of the Council on Library Resources. ∞

For Paul

The blood continuing on its rounds,
the heart stuck in its stutter of yes,
the brain still keeping its trillions
of mysterious appointments,
you with me, I with you—
what more is there to celebrate?

6/15/88

CONTENTS

I

MISSING THE DEAD

I miss the old scrawl on the viaduct,
the crazily dancing red letters: BIRD LIVES.
It's gone now, the wall as clean as forgetting.
I go home and put on a record,
Charlie Parker Live at the Blue Note.
Each time I play it, months or years apart,
the music emerges more luminous;
I never listened so well before.

I wish my parents had been musicians
and left me themselves transformed into sound,
or that I could believe in the stars
as the radiant bodies of the dead.
Then I could stand in the dark, pointing out
my mother and father to all
who did not know them, how they shimmer,
how they keep getting brighter
as we keep moving toward each other.

WHEN I AM ASKED

When I am asked
how I began writing poems,
I talk about the indifference of nature.

It was soon after my mother died,
a brilliant June day,
everything blooming.

I sat on a gray stone bench
in a lovingly planted garden,
but the daylilies were as deaf
as the ears of drunken sleepers
and the roses curved inward.
Nothing was black or broken
and not a leaf fell
and the sun blared endless commercials
for summer holidays.

I sat on a gray stone bench
ringed with the ingenue faces
of pink and white impatiens
and placed my grief
in the mouth of language,
the only thing that would grieve with me.

IN THE MUSEUM

What draws me over and over
to the seated Buddha
above the garden restaurant
where women, dressed like flowers,
go in and out?

I stand on the polished floor
looking up at his face,
the smile I can't interpret,
for which my language
of good and evil
is not sufficient.

JOY

Don't cry, it's only music,
someone's voice is saying;
no one you love is dying.

It's only music. And it was only spring,
the world's unreasoning body
run amok, like a saint's, with glory,
that overwhelmed a young girl
into unreasoning sadness.
Crazy, she told herself,
I should be dancing with happiness.

But it happened again. It happens
when we make bottomless love—
there follows a bottomless sadness
which is not despair
but its nameless opposite.
It has nothing to do with the passing of time.
It's not about loss. It's about
two seemingly parallel lines
suddenly coming together
inside us, in some place
that is still wilderness.

Joy, joy, the sopranos sing,
reaching for the shimmering notes
while our eyes fill with tears.

CAVALLERIA RUSTICANA

All the fireflies in the world
are gathered in our yard tonight,
flickering in the shrubs
like an ostentatious display
of Christmas lights out of season.
But the music in the air
is the music of heat, of August—
cicadas scraping out
their thin, harsh treble
like country fiddlers settling in
for a long night. I feel at home
with their relentless tune,
minimalist, like the Eighties.

Events repeat themselves,
but with a difference that makes all
the difference. As a child,
one summer night in Verona
at my first opera,
I watched a swarm of matches
light up the Roman arena
until we were silent. It was as if
music were a night-blooming flower
that would not open
until we held our breath.
Then the full-blown sound,
the single-minded combat
of passion: voices sharpening
their glittering blades on one another,
electing to live or die.
It was that simple. The story was
of no importance, the motive lost
in the sufficient, breathing dark.
If there was a moon I don't remember.

MAGNOLIA

This year spring and summer decided
to make it quick, roll themselves into one
season of three days
and steam right out of winter.
In the front yard the reluctant
magnolia buds lost control
and suddenly stood wide open.
Two days later their pale pink silks
heaped up around the trunk
like cast-off petticoats.

Remember how long spring used to take?
And how long from the first locking of fingers
to the first real kiss? And after that
the other eternity, endless motion
toward the undoing of a button?

FAMILY AND FRIENDS

We are sitting around the table
talking about the pros and cons
of adolescent rebellion.
We have been over this ground so often
we know all the potholes, the slippery spots.

Technology next, the computer as villain,
We play to each other, each word foreknown.
Not once does anyone lead the wrong suit.

The state of the Union, then and now.
Did Jefferson mean what he said?
Someone is doodling. Someone goes to the bathroom.
Someone else hears the coffee boil over.
Like a knot, attention
is coming apart all at once.

In the end it is music that saves us,
the Waldstein Sonata. We move
to couches and padded chairs,
rest our heads against pillows.
Petunias, blue velvet,
bloom in a bowl. For a long time
we listen and no one says anything.
When we do, our voices have changed.

LARGE JIGSAW PUZZLE

I.

I start with the sky, my primeval
big top, my tent, my canopy bed.
On this first day of the puzzle
it's blue with white streaks,
clouds gone vague
as smiles. Something green intrudes,
a treetop. I keep going
until I recognize it's a maple,
then try to quit for today,
but a bird's beak thrusts itself
suddenly into the scene,
and it's absurd to leave this beak
cut off from its delicate head
and the winged body that covers
an outsize, amplified heart.
God had it easier, six days
of strict, categorical order,
while here thing blends into thing,
no borders, and wherever I stop
something is left unfinished:
sky ragged, tree broken, bird
no good without its wings.

2.

Finished, it turns out
to be a back that mimics
the color of the sky,
a mitered hood suggesting
authority, dominion.

My magnifying lens
picks out black stripes that run
back from the eyes—
a bird with glasses—

and reveals the prehensile strength
in its gray claws, those toes
that clasp a twig the way
my wedding ring clasps my finger

and the abstract expressionist tail,
a new shade of blue, crossed
by black horizontal lines.

I give up the world for today
to look at this single bird,
this particular jay.

3.

Like an elevator, I move
directly downward, filling in
the smooth trunk of the maple,
and arrive at the pointed tips
of what a child called the hair of the earth
and Whitman said is perhaps
the handkerchief of the Lord.
Green, I want you green,
wrote Lorca. Among the green
are hundreds of yellow heads,
wheels with dozens of spokes,
baby suns that will age
into white globes crammed with stars
until they explode, fly apart
to form new constellations,
give us the future, next spring.

4.

Next spring! But the puzzle is now,
this spring, not yet finished.
I tell myself today
I'll complete the puzzle. I'll tame the world
by closing the borders, sealing the frame,
locking the difficult content
into a cage. After that
the pieces will fall into place.
I finish the edge of the sky,
turn the left corner, and work straight down
until I come to a willow branch
which demands I follow it to its dip
over a lake. Then the lakeshore
demands I explore it until I get caught
in a thicket of raspberry canes,
flowering tentacles, green and white.
By now I am back in the middle,
absorbed in the local order
of leaves and thorns and blossoms,
my vision confined to the limits
of a manageable patch,
the world at large still full of holes.

VISITING MY NATIVE
COUNTRY WITH MY
AMERICAN-BORN HUSBAND

I am as much of a stranger
in this particular town
as he is. But when we walk
along the Neckar, an old folk song
comes back to me and I sing it to him
without a slip. In the restaurant
I notice my voice and my gestures
are like those of the women around me.
He watches me change contours
in the polished concave of his spoon;
he stirs his coffee and I dissolve.
When I come back I look different,
while he remains what he is,
what he always was.

DOVES

A pair of mourning doves
lets us come within three feet.
They sit on the ground, in the garden,
close-nestled, smoky gray,
like a couple that has grown old
together. They don't even flutter
or make anxious, throaty sounds,
so different from the blackbirds,
toughs who suspect an enemy—
a squirrel or boy with a BB gun—
in each of us, who take no chances
and scream and swoop at us
in our lawnchairs or on our way
to the garbage can. The doves
sit still, like birds in fairy tales,
who are there to test us,
our decency, our innate
civility. If we're not careful
they will rise and fly to our shoulders
and ask to be taken in.

LATE HOURS

On summer nights the world
moves within earshot
on the interstate with its swish
and growl, an occasional siren
that sends chills through us.
Sometimes, on clear, still nights,
voices float into our bedroom,
lunar and fragmented,
as if the sky had let them go
long before our birth.

In winter we close the windows
and read Chekhov,
nearly weeping for his world.

What luxury, to be so happy
that we can grieve
over imaginary lives.

POEM FOR MY BIRTHDAY

I have stopped being the heroine
of my bad dreams. The melodramas
of betrayal and narrow escapes
from which I wake up grateful
for an unexciting life
are starring my troubled young friend
or one of my daughters. I'm not the one
who swims too far out to sea;
I am the one who waves from shore
vainly and in despair.
Life is what happens to someone else;
I stand on the sidelines and wring my hands.
Strange that my dreams should have accepted
the minor role I've been cast in
by stories since stories began.
Does that mean I have solved my life?
I'm still afraid in my dreams, but not for myself.
Fear gets rededicated
with a new stone that bears a needier name.

GREAT PERFORMANCES

Again this morning I have escaped
from the black box of sleep,
my hands and feet unbound,
my lungs ballooning,
celebrating their freedom;
you, escaped before me,
have already taken your bow in the sun
to the applause of the trees
in their fullness of summer.

Now that our acts of magic are numbered,
I recognize our genius,
wondering how we do it,
the daily performance in which we submit
to the locks of absolute darkness,
dying to ourselves,
and stand up stretching, nonchalant
as the great Houdini himself.

Houdini, the master, who made
our taken-for-granted escapes
fabulous, showed the world
how we climb out of our griefs
again and again and rise
from illness as if from a strongbox
dropped to the bottom of the sea.

What is he doing, lying
in a grave in New York City,
weighted down by the earth?
If even he, our legend,
could not trick death forever,
he should have made it his greatest show,
should have transformed himself

into a bird and taken off
for heaven, in full view,
so we could cheer his vanishing
behind the floodlit sky,
a final curtain held for him.

II

WEDNESDAYS

Each Wednesday afternoon
I cover myself with sunshine.
Stepping into the nursing home,
I set my relentless smile.
On Valentine's Day I wear red
and hand out artificial roses,
American Beauties. The old women
are dressed in young girls' colors,
pink and shimmery blue;
their immaculate hairdos rise
above the heads of their wheelchairs.

I work for the library. Today,
an afternoon in May,
I bring them books on the royal wedding,
outsize, with glossy photographs.
I look up this month's dates
of note: two Presidents born,
Truman and Kennedy;
the war in Europe ended
forty-four years ago.
I do not dwell on Memorial Day.
We talk about graduations
and high school proms, about maypoles
and lilies of the valley,
while down the hall a woman screams
the same word over and over.

Sometimes I read them stories
about trees that live for 2,000 years
and love that never dies.

BEDTIME STORY

The moon lies on the river
like a drop of oil.
The children come to the banks to be healed
of their wounds and bruises.
The fathers who gave them their wounds and bruises
come to be healed of their rage.
The mothers grow lovely; their faces soften,
the birds in their throats awake.
They all stand hand in hand
and the trees around them,
forever on the verge
of becoming one of them,
stop shuddering and speak their first word.

But that is not the beginning.
It is the end of the story,
and before we come to the end,
the mothers and fathers and children
must find their way to the river,
separately, with no one to guide them.
That is the long, pitiless part,
and it will scare you.

THE ART OF FORGETTING

Carlota and Maximilian
wanted to be allowed
to fall in love with Mexico,
as if history had a heart
and cared that they were young
and Maximilian liked
orange trees better than armies.
They reigned, a European
fairy tale emperor and empress
eating from golden plates
in a wilderness that beguiled them.
Three years. Then history flipped
its coin and slammed it down.

That was when they began,
Carlota's lapses, her erasures.
She wiped out the unbearable,
erased her husband's execution
and lived for sixty oblivious years
in an out-of-the-way palace,
her exclusive madhouse,
wondering vaguely each evening
why he did not join her for dinner.
Once every spring (so the story goes)
she walked to the dock with the little boat,
the kind used for an afternoon's outing,
and said in a young girl's voice,
"Tomorrow we leave for Mexico."

ORAL HISTORY

I will never forget the day
he finally came back to us,
still in his prison clothes;
how we carried his legs,
unused to walking, on our shoulders
and bent to kiss his scarred hands.
Many of us wept
when we looked at his martyred face,
our longtime icon, now
miraculously with us.
Then we grew still and waited
for his barely healed tongue
to speak to us of the future.

For once the knives in our pockets
did not itch, and our hands
were as clean as young grass.
That day we wanted only
the wafer he held out to us,
a new life without violence.

I remember the ringing sound,
a carillon, of our voices
joined in the song we could finally
sing out loud. I remember
how we cheered him
who was already scanning the crowd
for the quieter voices,
the eyes that asked questions,
the hands slow to come forward.

VIRTUOSI

In Memory of My Parents

People whose lives have been shaped
by history—and it is always tragic—
do not want to talk about it,
would rather dance, give parties
on thrift shop china. You feel
wonderful in their homes,
two leaky rooms, nests
they stowed inside their hearts
on the road into exile.
They know how to fix potato peelings
and apple cores so you smack your lips.

The words *start over again*
hold no terror for them.
Obediently they rise
and go with only a rucksack
or tote bag. If they weep,
it's when you're not looking.

To tame their nightmares, they choose
the most dazzling occupations,
swallow the flames in the sunset sky,
jump through burning hoops
in their elegant tiger suits.
Cover your eyes: there's one
walking on a thread
thirty feet above us—
shivering points of light
leap across her body,
and she works without a net.

THREE POEMS ABOUT THE VOICELESS

1.

The voiceless wear scarves pulled tight
across their mouths, like the woman
on the commuter train
with the huge eyes and olive skin.
No English. Somehow she conveyed
that she had paid before getting on,
but she had no ticket. The conductor said
he wanted her name and address
so the railroad could send her a bill.
Her eyes went wild; the conductor
was wearing a uniform.
She shook her head: no English!
Her eyes above the muffler
darted from corner to corner
with the frantic speed of any small thing
that's trapped and cannot find an exit.

2.

Sometimes the voiceless decide
to shield their eyes. At McDonald's
a man's hard gaze slides sideways
to check me out, and when I turn
the eyes go blank, freeze forward,
agates that have seen nothing.

On the bus it happens again,
different hair and clothes, same eyes;
secretive antennae
darting and gone, bars drawn
across the windows of the soul.

I stare at two missing children
on the poster above his head.
Their eyes are straight on me,
as if I were the camera
and trust still possible.

3.

I've seen one of the voiceless
borrow the voice of the saxophone.
He stands on a downtown street
on a wintry, dull afternoon
blowing his heart out. His heart
slides down the tube of his instrument
and comes out in a long, sweet note,
excruciating and breathless,
like the harrowing pleasure of sex.
A voice made human, a language
all of us, shoppers, browsers
and purse-snatchers, understand.

APOCRYPHAL STORY

Richard Speck was convicted of killing eight student
nurses in Chicago in 1957.

After his blackout, Richard Speck
came to in a bar. Richard Speck
heard people talking about the horror,
eight young women dead. Richard Speck
shook his head at the general madness
that seemed to be going around
like the common cold. Richard Speck
wondered about his lost day and the foreign
smell of his clothes. Richard Speck
looked up at the screen to see who was winning
and heard the announcer say his name.
"Police are looking for Richard Speck,"
the announcer said. "They are sure
he is the killer." Richard Speck
walked out of the bar feeling whole,
the missing piece of his life
recovered, order restored.

SCENARIOS

She always thinks it's only
her neighbor at the door,
but it's never her neighbor;
it's her child being carried in
between two policemen.
And when the telephone rings
it's not the voice she expected;
it's darker and she wonders
where she has heard it before.

Nothing like that ever happens
except on TV, you say,
but think of the false reports,
of the passenger on the casualty list
who wanders for years in the mountains
and returns to a wife who is happy
with someone else;
or the woman who starts a fire
in her lover's room
only to learn that the dead man
is a stranger who'd just moved in.

How do I know I'm protected
by a lifetime of assumptions?
When the doorbell rings
it may be the mailman with a letter.
"Sign here," he'll say. The letter
will tell me I'm not who I think I am,
that I have a different name,
and my signature is a forgery,
that my husband was never intended for me,
therefore I have no rights to my daughters
and must give them up.

Begin again, the letter ends,
clean slate, fresh start, new life,
but the instructions are missing.

PUBLIC SERVICE ANNOUNCEMENT

Three images flash on the screen:
Pasteur, busy with test tubes;
Hitler, right arm raised,
addressing a rally of brown-shirted men;
a white horse running through fields.
Then a fourth: a boy reading,
because this is National Library Week.
The boy has beautiful eyes.
They shine as he reads and listens
to the soundtrack in his head:
glass clanking, a roar from a crowd,
an exuberant whinny. I want
to knock on the screen and tell him
one of the three is not romance
and not yet history. I was there
when that one happened and I'm still alive.
The boy's eyes shine impartially.
Tonight he may dream of a cowboy
whose face looks like Pasteur's,
wearing a swastika on his shirt
and riding a snow-white horse
through undulating grasses
into a blood-red sunset.

THE ARTIST

The girl who never speaks
draws a horse like you've never seen,
a horse with feathers,
with eyes cut into diamonds
like the eyes of a bee,
with a tail of braided grasses
and a mane of waterfalls.
Its ears are lilies
and its nostrils homes for swallows,
but its fine hooves and ankles
are what they always were,
because there is no greater beauty.

Where she lives there are no horses,
but she has seen them in books
and watched them rear and whinny
on television. She understands
their patience, day after day,
in the land of the flies. In a dream
she encountered a solitary
blue horse in a field. He came close
and ate an apple out of her hand.

She draws him over and over
in absolute silence. She is afraid
language will fritter away the world,
its gleam and thunder,
its soft, curled lip,
the flying back which only
she dares to ride.

EPILEPSY, PETIT MAL

There are times, each day, when their child leaves them—
briefly, for half a minute perhaps—
though she remains standing among them
with the toy or book she is holding.
Her body goes stiff, her pupils lock in position.
She cannot see them. All they can do is wait
until she is given back to them.
Then they ask her where she has been
and she answers, surprised, that she has been with them
the whole time. But they don't believe her;
they think she guards some fantastic secret,
a momentary vision of heaven
so intense that it stuns her. They cannot believe
the alternative, which is nothing—
those mock-deaths, over and over, for nothing.

PAUL DELVAUX: *THE VILLAGE*
OF THE MERMAIDS

Oil on canvas, 1943

Who is that man in black, walking
away from us into the distance?
The painter, they say, took a long time
finding his vision of the world.

The mermaids, if that is what they are
under their full-length skirts,
sit facing each other
all down the street, more of an alley,
in front of their gray row houses.
They all look the same, like a fair-haired
order of nuns, or like prostitutes
with chaste, identical faces.
How calm they are, with their vacant eyes,
their hands in laps that betray nothing.
Only one has scales on her dusky dress.

It is 1943; it is Europe,
and nothing fits. The one familiar figure
is the man in black approaching the sea,
and he is small and walking away from us.

APHASIA

It's not only because the world
is coming apart that it no longer
offers itself to me
as an infinite dictionary
and speech takes back its most glamorous figures.
Something in me, an alteration
like liquid turning solid,
draws me to the photograph
of the country woman whose mouth
has become a straight, hard line,
a terse signal for closure.
I try to imagine her younger,
her mouth swelling and parting
into lips, her nearly opaque eyes
fluid with expectation.
Clearly the world has never
offered itself to her;
it has taken and taken until she became
empty and sealed. The habit of speech
is not like riding a bicycle,
something you never forget;
it dries up like the habit of tears,
like playfulness. Nothing in her face
gives me permission to speak for her,
even if I could.

MARY

Mary points to a fellow patient
in the nursing home and says
"She's always crying." The woman
is weeping bitterly.
I'm shocked because there's no hint
of compassion in Mary's face.
"The callousness of the old," I think.
But then I realize that's not it.
Mary, deaf and in a wheelchair,
claims no more sympathy for herself,
accepts the world's indifference
as the natural order of things,
though her eyes still recognize kindness.
Death won't let anyone off the hook,
whether we rage or go gentle.
Mary's way is to let go,
little by little, of anger and love,
the self's constituents. She moves
toward death the way a swimmer
eases into freezing water:
ankles, knees, hips,
shivering ribcage, collarbone.

HEARTBREAK

It's in the farthest reaches that
the symptoms show: a peculiar
stiffening of the shoulders,
a new slump where blouse and skirt meet,
the way the feet come down hard
in your determinedly long stride.

Here, in the outposts of the heart,
the exile islands, grief plays itself out,
and here, my darling, it will begin to mend
long before the ailing ruler
in the capital knows what is happening.

AFTER YOUR DEATH

The first time we said your name
you broke through the flat crust of your grave
and rose, a movable statue,
walking and talking among us.

Since then you've grown a little.
We keep you slightly larger
than life-size, reciting bits of your story,
our favorite odds and ends.
Of all your faces we've chosen one
for you to wear, a face wiped clean
of sadness. Now you have no other.

You're in our power. Do we
terrify you, do you wish
for another face? Perhaps
you want to be left in darkness.

But you have no say in the matter.
As long as we live, we keep you
from dying your real death,
which is being forgotten. We say,
we don't want to abandon you,
when we mean, *we can't let you go.*

ALL NIGHT

All through the night the knot in the shoelace
waits for its liberation
and the match on the table packs its head
with anticipation of light.
The faucet sweats out a bead of water
which gathers strength for the free-fall,
while the lettuce in the refrigerator
succumbs to its brown killer.
And in the novel I put down
the paneled walls of a room
are condemned to stand and wait
for tomorrow, when I'll get to the page
where the prisoner finds the secret door
and steps into air and the scent of lilacs.

COSTUME

A few weeks before Halloween a local theater is selling some of its old costumes, among them a dress worn by a famous actress when she played Hedda Gabler. I think of the woman who buys that dress, pleased with her find, ready for the party. When she goes home and tries it on, she straightens up and grows taller. She decides she must have her hair done in a new way. At the salon, she is different with her hairdresser, less talkative, more distant. On the way home she picks up some groceries and has them put in her car, even though the bag is light. She performs a gesture, new to her, that causes the grocery boy to look up in admiration. That evening she discovers her husband is a clod, a dull little man without imagination. How had she not seen it before? During the week she calls up an old lover, and they meet. They meet again; several times; it's all in fun, you understand, no strings, no commitment. She is not one to take risks. But she must do something to break the boredom of her dull job, dull marriage, the predictable remarks of her friends. She eats less and exercises more; her husband doesn't notice how thin she is getting, how easily she flies off the handle. Some time after the Halloween party she buys a pistol. *For protection,* she tells her husband, *there have been so many break-ins in this neighborhood.*

PLEASE STAND BY

With the sound off, they look like us when we dream. They smile and nod, engaging in mimed conversation. Then their faces tighten. Her mouth opens in a soundless cry. He crosses his arms and turns away; she lifts her hands, two severed wings. No other motions are possible. They move through a life of gestures that make no sense and cannot be altered. They are like fish in a tank whose mouths flap open and shut. But they are not fish; they are people who don't understand that they understand nothing. They don't know they are in despair because they are without imagination. Just when I think I can't bear to watch them any longer the sound returns. Awake, they instantly become difficult, asking for reasons and refusing actions they have not chosen.

THE DEAF DANCING TO ROCK

The eardrums of the deaf are already broken; they like it loud. They dance away the pain of silence, of a world where people laugh and wince and smirk and burst into tears over words they don't understand. As they dance the world reaches out to them, from the floor, from the vibrating walls. Now they hear the ongoing drone of a star in its nearly endless fall through space; they hear seedlings break through the crust of the earth in split-second thumps, and in another part of the world, the thud of billions of leaves hitting the ground, apart and together, in the intricate rhythmic patterns we cannot hear. Their feet, knees, hips, enact the rhythms of the universe. Their waving arms signal the sea and pull its great waves ashore.

MOULIN ROUGE

The feminine form for clown seems to be
clownesse; that's what it says beneath
my print of Toulouse-Lautrec's
The Clownesse Cha-U-Kao.
She is a fake, of course,
blond, and lacking Asian features.
Nor is her lovely face insulted
by a red nose, and the ruffles feathering
bosom and shoulders are chic. A fool,
in other words, in the Shakespearean sense,
a gracefully sharp-tongued teller
of shocking truths. But what ruler
would permit such a role for a woman,
a *foolesse,* even if she danced for him?

Say this woman had outrageous dreams.
Say that, each night, she searched the posh crowd
for the right face, a balding man's,
sensual and cocksure,
and played to him as a Chinese warlord;
that she danced at his table and sang
a macabre, side-splitting song
about a beheaded despot
and a woman who took his head
and rolled it along the street like a hoop.

FILM SCRIPT

A tall, redheaded woman
in a green shirt and white slacks
is walking along a deserted beach.
Her life has become a cruel riddle;
she thinks she may find the answer
in the sky or the sand. As she walks,
a bottle washes up before her
bare feet. She stoops and opens it,
pulls out the message. Staggers.
Stuffs it back in the bottle
and throws it out to sea,
a long, fierce, overhand throw.
Her face is pure terror. She turns around
and walks in the direction she came from,
as if there was still a chance to catch up
with her old life. She does not feel
the broken shells and slippery seaweed.
The sky maintains its bluish face
with the few bland summer clouds;
the sea remains placid. She feels herself
becoming lighter, losing ground;
her sandals drop from her hand,
her feet stop touching the sand. She is rising,
slowly at first. Her contours blur,
dissolve at the edges until she becomes
a low-lying cloud, a delicate shred of fog
that finally fills with consuming light,
and she is lost, like breath given back to the air.

LOST AND FOUND

The gold ring is lost; it lies
at the bottom of the river.
But never mind; one day
a magnificent fish will swallow it
and the royal fisherman
will bring the fish to the surface
for the cook to poach whole
and deliciously seasoned. At dinner,
on a white plate, it will open
like a purse to reveal the ring.

That's where the story starts:
how it was dropped, and why
it was so important.
A life unrolls from the gold token,
cumulative as a landslide—
how poor and young and hopeful
he was at the time, and how foolish,
but how luck was with him
and the beautiful woman stayed,
and so began the pile of days
that heap around them like October.

And what if the ring is not found?
Ah, then the story is lost
because no one remembers to tell it.
This is the joke, the cruel one—
that memory, all the past we have,
should fasten to such tenuous things:
a ring, a receipt, a dimly recognized button,
a nail driven into a plaster wall
at a certain slant.

THIS WINTER

Each morning I used to open my eyes
to the top of a dead elm.
It had no leaves, of course—
in fact, it was as bare
as a clothes pole for twenty years—
but it served as the favorite lookout for crows.
I used to watch them watch out for each other
in their ravenous search for anything,
dead or alive, that's good to eat.
So smart, so loyal. And then there was
the loner, the one I thought of
as Schubert's crow, his traveler's only companion
on the heartbreaking walk through winter,
that long abandonment which breaks off
without any blessing of thaw
in the hard rivers. My recording of this
is too sad to play, has become sadder
with every death. But the crow,
the real, live thing without music or meaning,
black, rough-voiced, unfailing,
was there for me too, certain as sunrise.
This winter the tree has collapsed,
gently, a gradual letting go,
the way the dead loosen their hold
on the living. When I open my eyes,
the window frames a piece of sky
vague as a snapshot from a vacationer's
small instamatic—where was that?
Occasionally a bird flies through,
a finch or dove, but it doesn't stay,
having no place to settle down.

TRIAGE

Bertolt Brecht lamented that he lived in an age when it was almost a crime to talk about trees, because that meant being silent about so much evil. Walking past a stand of tall, still healthy elms along Chicago's lakefront, I think of what Brecht said. I want to celebrate these elms which have been spared by the plague, these survivors of a once flourishing tribe commemorated by all the Elm Streets in America. But to celebrate them is to be silent about the people who sit and sleep underneath them, the homeless poor who are hauled away by the city like trash, except it has no place to dump them. To speak of one thing is to suppress another. When I talk about myself, I cannot talk about you. You know this as you listen to me, disappointment settling in your face.

MUSE

What I look at when I type is a poster: Edward Hopper's *Night-hawks*. It is there to keep me honest. I look at a couple having coffee in a diner late at night; their relationship is ambiguous; she looks fragile, vulnerable, no longer quite young; his forehead is shad-owed by the wide brim of his hat. Their faces are bleached by the merciless light. The gaunt-faced waiter leans forward; he wants to tell them about himself. They are someone to talk to in this plate-glass house with the redundant salt and pepper shakers, the care-fully spaced chrome napkin holders. The man apart, whose back is to me, is a mystery. Forty-five years ago, when Hopper painted these people, did he know they would endure? I see them down-town in the underground concourse below the glass hotel and the granite-and-marble bank; in that spooky region lined with over-priced shops selling cheap goods, and drab cafes tarted up with lights. There they are, no older, only he is hatless these days. The waiter-turned-waitress is still thin-faced and can't support her kids on what she makes. And the loner sits in the corner and faces me now, but his face might as well be a back.

SLIDES

My friend has no wish to travel. "I don't have to visit Las Vegas," he says, "I already know what it's like." Yes, and what the Sistine Chapel is like, and the Amazon jungles, the faces of Everest and the Hall of Mirrors at Versailles, though he hasn't visited any of them. His head, like everyone else's, is a museum of places he has not been to, filled with color slides. He owns the Grand Canyon, the rock star's mansion, the treatment center where the First Lady was cured of alcoholism, the Great Wall of China. The only place he can't flatten into a two-dimensional image is the house that surrounds him: the gleaming bathtub that could turn treacherous; the kitchen filled to exploding with years of talk; the bed upstairs, at the moment pristine, tucked-in, that gives no hint of its intentions.

BRENDEL PLAYING SCHUBERT

We bring our hands together
in applause, that absurd noise,
when we want to be silent. We might as well
be banging pots and pans,
it is that jarring, a violation
of the music we've listened to
without moving, almost holding our breath.
The pianist in his blindingly
white summer jacket bows
and disappears and returns
and bows again. We keep up
the clatter, so cacophonous
that it should signal revenge
instead of the gratitude we feel
for the two hours we've spent
out of our bodies and away
from our guardian selves
in the nowhere where the enchanted live.

ROMANTICS

Johannes Brahms and Clara Schumann

The modern biographers worry
"how far it went," their tender friendship.
They wonder just what it means
when he writes he thinks of her constantly,
his guardian angel, beloved friend.
The modern biographers ask
the rude, irrelevant question
of our age, as if the event
of two bodies meshing together
establishes the degree of love,
forgetting how softly Eros walked
in the nineteenth century, how a hand
held overlong or a gaze anchored
in someone's eyes could unseat a heart,
and nuances of address not known
in our egalitarian language
could make the redolent air
tremble and shimmer with the heat
of possibility. Each time I hear
the Intermezzi, sad
and lavish in their tenderness,
I imagine the two of them
sitting in a garden
among late-blooming roses
and dark cascades of leaves,
letting the landscape speak for them,
leaving us nothing to overhear.

NOCTURNE

Sometimes, in the dead of night, I wake up in an immense hole of silence. Then I wait, with hope and dread, for the first sound to drop into it. Hope for something benign: the soothing background music of rain, or an owl's throaty signal. Dread of a wailing siren, or the telephone, which at this hour could bring me only a thick, demented voice, or the impersonal speech issuing from some desk of disaster. Last night, when it came, it was a sound of blessing, the rough-and-tumble bumping together of freight cars in the switch-yard down the road—that simple, artless coupling, and a long time later, the drawn-out, low-voiced hum of the train rolling down the single track. Sounds of work, of confidence in the night, in getting from here to there. Sounds of connection; sweet music. I lay there and listened to the moonless night fill up with sound until the darkness throbbed with a dream of arrival.